MW01284007

# Finding Yourself

*Discover How to Find Yourself, Define Yourself, and Pave Your Own Path into the Future*

by Ian Branneth

# Table of Contents

# Introduction

Feeling stuck, are you? Things seem to be happening to everyone else, just not to you? Others are getting on with their lives, but you seem to have missed the bus?

Or perhaps you're just lacking clarity as to what exactly you want out of life anymore?

Or wait: You're where you've always wanted to be, but it's just not quite living up to what you expected, or it's no longer satisfying for some reason – is that it?

Barring hormones, overwork, exhaustion, drugs (prescribed, legal, other otherwise), you're probably unsure about a lot of things right now. The only thing you seem to know for sure, is that you don't like wherever it is that you are, and yet you don't know exactly what to do about it.

Worse yet, you have way too many ideas as to what you could be doing that you're too overwhelmed to act – paralyzed in a sense.

Or doubly worse, you have absolutely no clue what to do about your situation.

Assuming you're not languishing in jail or stuck at the bottom of a dirt pit, there's one thing you can take comfort in: The feeling of being stuck is just that - it's a *feeling*, an emotional condition. It is **not** a fact, and it is **not** something inherent in you or your environment.

To further clarify this point: No one is denying that the circumstances in your life have made you feel stuck. Perhaps the bills are mounting and you don't know how to keep up. Perhaps you're about to get kicked out of your house. Perhaps you've been with the same company for ten years in the same position and with the same pay. Perhaps the zing has disappeared from your relationship and you want to leave, but you can't or won't or don't want to deal with it. Perhaps there's nothing physically wrong with you and you're not tired, but the thought of getting out of bed in the morning leaves you with a feeling of resignation, or one of horror and dread.

Yes? Uh-huh. So there you go. See? It's emotional.

**Now I've got some GOOD NEWS for you:**

This book is designed to help you regain control of your emotional state of being, and help you identify (and get on) the path that you were meant to walk. You'll learn how to effectively face your mental rut with various exercises, and how to get a grip on the root cause of your current situation so you can better deal with it and freely move forward with your life again. Let's stop wallowing in your perceived misfortune, and let's get started fixing it!

© Copyright 2015 by Miafn LLC - All rights reserved.

This document is geared towards providing reliable information in regards to the topic and issue covered. The publication is sold with the idea that the publisher is not required to render accounting, officially permitted, or otherwise, qualified services. If advice is necessary, legal or professional, a practiced individual in the profession should be ordered.

- From a Declaration of Principles which was accepted and approved equally by a Committee of the American Bar Association and a Committee of Publishers and Associations.

In no way is it legal to reproduce, duplicate, or transmit any part of this document in either electronic means or in printed format. Recording of this publication is strictly prohibited and any storage of this document is not allowed unless with written permission from the publisher. All rights reserved.

The information provided herein is stated to be truthful and consistent, in that any liability, in terms of inattention or otherwise, by any usage or abuse of any policies, processes, or directions contained within is solely and completely the responsibility of the recipient reader. Under no circumstances will any legal responsibility or blame be held against the publisher for any reparation, damages, or monetary loss due to the information herein, either directly or indirectly.

Respective authors own all copyrights not held by the publisher.

The information herein is offered for informational purposes solely, and is universal as so. The presentation of the information is without contract or any type of guarantee assurance.

The trademarks that are used are without any consent, and the publication of the trademark is without permission or backing by the trademark owner. All trademarks and brands within this book are for clarifying purposes only and are the owned by the owners themselves, not affiliated with this document.

# Chapter 1: Just How Stuck Are You?

Only you can answer that question. Most people try to run away from such questions because they can be overwhelming. Others think that admitting to being stuck somehow means they've failed. Still others think that if they just carry on and ignore their rut, it'll somehow go away. Some become so successful at denial that they don't even realize there's a problem.

Most know they're stuck or lost because they feel depressed, desperate, empty, helpless, hopeless, and trapped. In extreme cases, they feel a strong sense of self-loathing and believe that life isn't worth living. According to the experts, these last two are very serious, so if you feel this bad, get yourself professional help right away.

It doesn't always manifest in such clear-cut emotional terms, unfortunately. Other signs include sudden mood swings, drastic weight change, loss of appetite, insomnia or too much sleep, irritability, aggression, an inability to focus, reckless behavior, constant exhaustion or lack of energy, as well as increased aches and pains (including headaches).

Whatever the case, it helps to first acknowledge that there might be a problem. If you can't or won't share your situation with others, then start with yourself. A good way to begin is through journaling.

For some the idea of writing down their thoughts is a daunting task, but it doesn't have to be. Since diaries are personal things, you don't have to worry about grammar and spelling. All you have to worry about is venting your feelings and developing a tool for keeping better tabs on yourself.

Recently, brain scans on those who keep diaries found that they were generally happier, better adjusted people than those who didn't. Neuropsychologists found that committed diarists show less active amygdalae—the almond-shaped forms between the two hemispheres of our brain which regulate the intensity of our emotions.

They call it the Bridget Jones Effect. Doesn't matter if you write your thoughts down in a diary, compose poems, or invent song lyrics. The act of recording your thoughts and emotions regularly allows your brain to develop better emotional control and maintain better emotional equilibrium, as a result. They also found that this benefits men more than women—probably because women are generally more comfortable about sharing their thoughts and feelings with others. In other words, women already have a head start on men in this area.

Perhaps you already know why you're lost or stuck. By keeping a journal, however, you can gain a better insight into your situation and hopefully, work your way out of it more quickly.

Think of your diary as a kind of map in progress. If you're lost or stuck, it's a way of knowing where you are so you can take the steps needed to find your way back home.

# Chapter 2: Why and How to Keep a Journal

The therapeutic benefits of journaling are so highly recognized in the medical profession that this bit needs to be covered. It was in the 1960s that Dr. Ira Progoff first proposed the method that is today called Journal Therapy.

You can write anything in your diary, from your thoughts and feelings, to how your day went, and yes, even song lyrics and poetry. What makes Dr. Progoff's method so different, however, is that he asks you to write things from a very personal point of view.

If your day went badly, for example, don't just list the things that went wrong. Explain what you felt as they happened, how you reacted, and what you felt as a result. You don't have to explain yourself if you don't want to; you don't even have to understand or delve deeper into your feelings if you're not up to it. Simply explain what you felt and what you reacted to.

When dealing with extremely emotional issues that make you uncomfortable, you can use the third person. Rather than write: "I felt bad about that," you can instead write: "s/he felt bad about that."

To maximize the benefits of journaling, try to devote 10 minutes a day to it. If possible, try to do it at the same time and in the same place so you can get into the right mood for it. The best times are in the morning before work and in the evening before bed.

Once you write, don't stop. As cited in the previous chapter, this is a personal thing, so you don't have to worry about spelling and grammar. You don't even have to make sense. Your aim is to just write and let things flow. This includes not censoring yourself.

If you get stuck with writer's block, write about something that's been on your mind lately, an imaginary dialogue you want to have with someone, a fantasy or a goal, a dream you recently had, etc. You can also use your diary to brainstorm ideas, devise plans, write out to-do lists, or even whine and gripe about something or someone.

Making a regular session of your journaling also helps you develop discipline and self-awareness, two things that'll be discussed in greater detail later. It also helps you keep track of your progress, identify weaknesses and self-destructive patterns which could be dragging you down, and better appreciate your own strengths in case you forgot about them.

To be a successful diarist, you need to (1) make a habit of it, (2) be honest with yourself, (3) not be overly concerned about what you'll write, and (4) not worry too much about what others will think (or what you think they will). To avoid the latter altogether, try to keep your diary in a safe place away from prying eyes.

For many, the habit of journaling is enough to help them find their way. For most, it's a tool that helps to get them started. So you might want to start now.

# Chapter 3: Finding the Power of Your Own Breath

Taking a deep breath can do wonders for you. Try it right now. See? This is why people take a deep breath before giving a speech, breaking bad news to others, or doing something they're not too happy about.

Doing so in no way changes the situation, whatsoever, but it does allow your mind to calm down a bit and to take a step back from the turmoil you're feeling. If you pay close attention, you'll notice that the more tense you are, the quicker and shallower your breathing becomes. The more relaxed you are the slower and deeper your breathing tends to be.

There's an actual science behind this. Our emotional state is tied to our breath because we depended on it for our survival. In the prehistoric past, fear and stress meant we were in danger. When taking in quick, shallow breaths, our brain goes on high alert, the blood pumps faster through our veins, our muscles become tenser, and we can either run from the danger or stay and fight it.

Today, however, things are a little more complicated. Our world has changed, but our body's autonomic responses have stayed the same; hence the modern phenomenon of stress-related diseases. You can't run away from the IRS, nor can you (or should you) beat up your boss or overly-aggressive telemarketers. And though the weekend brings some relief, the knowledge that the whole grind will start again on Monday brings no relief, whatsoever.

So take a deep breath. When you do, you stimulate your vagus nerve. This in turn tells your heart rate to slow down. When it does, a signal gets sent to your brain to stop flooding your body with the neurochemicals that gets it pumped and primed for action, so you relax and slow down.

Now here's the thing. Most people breathe wrong. If you pay attention to your breathing, there's a good chance that you're breathing only into your chest. If your shoulders rise and fall then that's exactly what you're doing—breathing wrong. Breathing this way does not maximize oxygen intake, nor is it effective at ridding your lungs of accumulated toxins.

The correct way to breathe is the way infants and toddlers do it before they grow up—with the belly.

To breathe this way, first relax your chest and shoulders. Now take the breath down into your belly so that it bloats when you inhale. When you exhale, pull your stomach in.

Try it. Sit up straight and breathe into your belly. If your shoulders rise and fall, you're still doing it wrong. Practice till your breathing creates a natural in-and-out movement of your belly, while keeping your shoulders and chest relaxed. This is called abdominal breathing and can do wonders for your health, your state of mind, and your stress levels.

The next time you feel down, stressed, or confused, breathe deep into your belly.

# Chapter 4:   Starting a Simple and Effective Meditation Practice

Unless you're an Amish or a Luddite, chances are that you've been hearing about the mental and physical benefits of meditation. Modern science and medicine has proven that meditation is a powerful tool for helping people with depression, post-traumatic stress disorder, and a whole host of other psychological problems. Meditation can also help you get over that "stuck" feeling.

There are many meditative practices out there, but one of the simplest is called vipassana—which is Pali for "inward vision." Vipassana is a way of focusing your mind on your breath and on your bodily sensations. With practice, you develop certain mental and physical insights about yourself.

To do it, simply sit still and upright. You don't have to sit on the floor with your legs crossed if that's not your thing. A stool or bench will do, but don't lean back on anything like a wall or a back rest. The need to constantly adjust your posture so you remain upright is an important part of this exercise.

If you sit on a stool, make sure to keep your feet flat on the ground. Don't cross your ankles or rest one leg on the other because the former will unbalance you, while the latter will create pressure that'll make the other leg fall asleep. You want to find a posture you can maintain comfortably without moving for at least five minutes. Rest your hands on your lap, but don't cross them or let them dangle at your sides because that'll eventually create strain on your shoulders.

Make a slight arch with your spine so your shoulders lean back slightly and keep your head upright. Feel free to make whatever adjustments you need, so long as your spine remains straight and you're comfortable. Now close your eyes.

The first thing you have to do is to inhale deeply, allowing your belly to expand, and then exhale only through your nose, not your mouth. Make sure your breathing is natural and comfortable, without strain or tension. You should also try to make your in-breath equal to your out-breath. Don't inhale deeply then follow it up with a short exhalation. Simply breathe as you normally would, but abdominally instead of with your chest.

Keep your primary focus on your breathing. If you feel other sensations like itching, let a part of your mind zoom in on the spot, but keep your main focus on breathing in and out. Observe the itch, where it is on your body, how intense it is, how focused or diffuse it is, etc., but don't react. If you do this long enough, the itch will fade. You can do this with aches, tension, and other bodily sensations.

When it comes to thoughts, images, and memories, however, try not to engage them. It's easy and tempting to follow those trains of thought, but in vipassana, your aim is to stay focused on your breath and body. Rather than entertain those thoughts, simply acknowledge that your mind is wandering then get back to your breathing. With enough practice, those mental distractions will become less and less, until your sole focus remains on your breathing. Try to do this for at least five minutes a day. Ten is better.

# Chapter 5: The Law of Dependent Arising

This comes from Buddhist philosophy, which has had a major impact on Asian thought. You don't have to know anything about Asia or Buddhism, but the Law of Dependent Arising provides a useful framework in understanding how and why we think, feel, and act as we do.

According to the Law of Dependent Arising, no object, person, condition, phenomenon, thought, or action has an independent existence. You exist because of your parents; trees exist because of earth, water, nutrients, and sunlight; shade exists because of light; the Civil Rights Movement began because African-Americans got tired of being ill-treated; and so on.

Nothing, in other words, comes into being out of nothing. Everything exists because of something else and everything that exists is dependent on something else. In the *Saṃyuktāgama* (a Buddhist text) it's written that:

*"This exists so that exists,*
*This brings about that*
*Without this, that is not*
*This disappears and that disappears."*


You were not always lost or uncertain. Innocent? Yes. Ignorant? Certainly. But the feeling of being out of whack and cast adrift was not always there. Certain conditions brought it about. Those conditions are sometimes clear to you, but not always.


Yet even when the causes are known, the solutions are not always obvious. The word "solutions" is not used here to refer to a set of actions. It refers instead to the emotional frame of mind required to act correctly.


Alcoholics know they're ruining their lives, for example, and that the proper thing to do is to abstain from alcohol. Knowing what to do is one thing, but having the emotional strength or willpower to actually do it is a different issue. This is why some people keep ending up in the same dead-end job, the same dead-end relationships, and the same dead-end situations.

If the Law of Dependent Origination is correct, then people repeat the same mistakes over and over again because they're focusing on the effect not the cause. And if you can't seem to break out of your emotional funk, then maybe it's because you're not addressing the real reasons behind it.

"This exists so that exists," if "this disappears [then] that disappears," how do you find "this" to get rid of "that?" By paying very close attention to yourself.

Journaling is one way. Meditation is another. Assuming you've gotten comfortable with vipassana, you can take things up another notch and dig a little deeper.

# Chapter 6: Focusing on the Body

You can do this after a meditation session, but it's really not necessary. What you need is to be in a place where you won't be bothered for a few minutes. You can even do this on the toilet or during a commute. Just don't do it if you're driving, alright?

Stress, emotional problems, and mental discomfort have physical counterparts in the body. This usually manifests as tension in the neck, shoulders, chest, and stomach, though not always simultaneously.

According to yoga, information is not just stored in the head. It's also stored in the body as well as through specific postures. If you're upset about something, you generate emotional energy which gets stored in parts of your body. By knowing where that energy gets stored, you can release it. In doing so, you undo emotional turmoil and achieve the calm and logical state of mind needed to deal with the causes of your problems more effectively.

The next time you feel stressed out or upset over something, stop for a moment and take a deep breath. Now pay attention to your body. Is your jaw clenched? Are your hands wadded up into fists? Is your stomach in knots? Are your shoulders aching? Is your face flushed? All of the above?

Focus on the spot or spots. Let's say your chest is tense and your stomach is knotted up, for example. Which is more tense, your chest or your stomach? Let's say your stomach is upset. Focus on your stomach. Is the tension located in any particular part of your stomach or is it more diffuse? Can you say if it's hard or semi-hard? Does it feel as if you just got punched or as if you ate something you shouldn't have?

Are you sure it's just localized in your stomach? Does the discomfort extend to your legs, groin, and back? Can you associate the discomfort with a texture, a color, or even a temperature?

If you say your stomach is in a knot, how hard is that knot? Does it feel like a tight knot or a loose one? Does it feel thick or thin? Dark or light? Is it in the center of your abdomen or is it more to the left or right? Perhaps higher up in your solar plexus? Or lower down closer to your groin? If the discomfort extends to your chest, apply the same analysis to your chest.

Do not focus on the causes of your emotional discomfort, do not analyze why you feel as you do, nor should you try to suppress your feelings. Your aim is to focus on how your body is feeling and to what degree it feels the way it does.

Do not, in other words, try to suppress or run away from your discomfort. Face it squarely and bravely, but do so analytically from a physical perspective. Don't say, "I'm an adult, I shouldn't feel this way." Instead, acknowledge that you feel something and explore it. You'll find that the more you face your discomfort, the more it tends to fade.

# Chapter 7: Understanding Diffuse Emotions

Sometimes, you feel off whack but can't exactly explain why. All you know is that you're feeling off your game. In such cases, your body is again your best friend. What you don't consciously know, your body does on a subconscious level.

To get to the bottom of why you're feeling as you are, sit as you would in vipassana. Spend a few minutes focusing on your breath. Now breathe into your toes.

You do this by imagining your toes expanding as your belly does with each in-breath and by imagining your toes deflating as your belly does with each out-breath. Do this for a minute or two (or even three), then work your way up your calves, your upper legs, your thighs, your groin, your buttocks, your chest, lower and upper back, shoulders, upper and lower arms, wrists, hands, neck, face, ears, then the back and the top of your head.

It sounds stupid, but it's a great way to let you know if there's discomfort or tension in any part of your body. Often, our bodies tell us a lot of things through itchiness, tension, strain, pain, numbness, etc. But because our minds are often distracted by other things, we become desensitized to these messages, sometimes until it's too late.

If you feel a little off kilter, that emotion will definitely manifest itself in some part of your body. Once you identify where it is, you can begin to address it more effectively. Again, it's usually in your stomach, chest, and shoulders, but sometimes, it can also manifest in the hands, arms, legs, and feet, as well as the head.

Barring dehydration, head injuries, sinusitis, a poor diet, and medication, unresolved emotional issues also manifest as migraines and headaches. If you get a headache, try to isolate the pain by focusing on it.

Where on your head is it? Is it an intense throbbing or is it more of a dull ache? Does it feel as if someone were smashing that bit of your head in or as if they were drilling a hole through? Is it just on your head, or does the pain extend elsewhere, like your neck and shoulders? Can you associate the pain with a color, texture, or temperature?

The more you develop sensitivity to your body's messages, the more sensitive you become to your emotions and state of mind. As with the previous exercises, do not try to run away from the physical sensations by drugging yourself with pain killers. You can get to those later, but unless you develop the discipline needed to face discomfort and pain, you run the risk of letting those emotional issues build up.

Please note that this is not to denigrate your GP or to get you off whatever medication has been prescribed for you, if any. Nor is this an attempt to condemn any form of self-medication you like to engage in, if at all. This is simply an exercise to help you get in touch with any unresolved emotional issues that may have been building up. And if you are a normal human being, then you most certainly have them. So now what?

# Chapter 8: Identifying the Underlying Issues

Once you've found those bits of itchiness, tension, numbness, etc., you've won half your battle. Psychotherapy has lost much of its credibility, but focusing is gaining ground because a growing number of clinical studies are proving that it works. In doing so, it saves people thousands of dollars because they no longer have to spend years on therapy which gets them absolutely nowhere.

This does not mean that psychology or psychiatry doesn't work. Even the professionals admit that it's not what they do that helps their patients, instead it's what goes on inside their patients.

Putting vipassana and focusing together works like this. Say you feel your life is going nowhere, but you don't know if you should quit your job, join a circus, or maybe just take a long vacation but aren't sure if you can afford to. Before you sink into an existentialist crisis, sit in vipassana, instead. Now breathe into different parts of your body.

If that itchiness, tension, ache, etc., is simply the result of your posture or the fabric of your clothes, focusing on them will make them go away. If those sensations are the result of an emotional component, however, maintaining your focus on that sensation will bring that emotion to the fore.

Let's say you find your chest tightening up a bit. If you focus on that tension and it doesn't go away, stick with it. Find out how intense that tension is, how localized it is, if it spreads to other parts of your body, etc. If that tension has an emotional component, staying focused on it will bring that emotion up. It could be fear, anger, resignation, excitement, and so on.

While maintaining your focus on the physical sensation, let another part of your mind rest on the emotions that well up. Do not try to repress those emotions, rationalize them, or seek to understand them. Just let them come.

Often, one emotion will lead to another. Let those come out, as well. Often, because unresolved emotional issues build up, there are layers and layers of them stored in different parts of our bodies. When they become too much, they result in a sort of emotional paralysis which makes it difficult to act.

Allowing these to come out begins an emotional cathartic process which often frees you from the paralysis which holds you in place.

You can also use this exercise for dealing with issues that are bothering you. Let's say you feel stuck, for example. Sit in vipassana for a few minutes then mentally tell yourself, "I feel stuck."

Don't explain why, don't provide justifications, nor try to pontificate. Don't say, "I feel stuck because…" or "My financial/professional/relationship situation makes me feel stuck…" Knowing the causes of your problem and being able to do something about them are completely different things. We are dealing here with the emotional component needed to act properly.

When you say you feel stuck (or lost, or overwhelmed, or adrift, etc.), what part of your body reacts the most? Begin focusing on that portion, or those portions, and start identifying what it feels like. The physical sensations will come first, followed by the emotions. If you can identify them (sad, happy, excited, tense, nervous, etc.), then do so, but don't strain yourself.

You want to experience the physical sensations, but you don't want to get in the way of the outpouring of emotions. You'll find that in most cases, the emotions take a while to come to the fore. They'll feel like an itch somewhere you can't locate right away. The moment you scratch the spot you think the itch is coming from, it appears elsewhere.

At other times, it comes right away. When it does, it's usually an outpouring that can sometimes be overwhelming. Often, it goes away after a few minutes, but sometimes (in very rare cases), it can take days to get through. If there are many emotions stored up, they often come one after another. If you feel sad when you focus on a spot and it fades, wait a moment to make sure another one isn't still buried there somewhere.

Those who master the ability to focus describe it as being similar to forgetting something. Ever stepped out of your house only to realize you've forgotten something but haven't a clue as to what it is? Sometimes, you're too far away to go back home, so you fret and wrack your brain wondering what you've forgotten. When it finally hits you—maybe you forgot to turn off the porch light—you say, "Aha!" and feel a sense of relief.

You still can't go back home right away, you still can't turn off the light, and you'll still pay for it when the bill comes at the end of the month. But there's that immediate sense of physical and mental relief that you've finally gotten to the root of the problem.

That knowing releases a sort of tension in your gut which has an emotional and mental component to it. It creates an "aha, so that's it!" moment which brings about a sense of mental and emotional resolution.

# Conclusion

Sometimes, even you don't know why you're lost or stuck. Fortunately, your body and mind always do. By learning to meditate and to focus, you can hone in on the wisdom of your mind and body to get to the bottom of your mental and emotional issues.

Knowing won't solve the problem, per se. But just as knowing you left the light on (even if you can't shut it off right away) brings relief, so will knowing your own issues do the same.

Sometimes, the issues which hold you back can also propel you forward—but only if you identify them first. When you learn to do this, you can untangle yourself from the layers you've buried yourself under. Then and only then can you take the first steps toward finding yourself and charting a better path toward a future of your own choosing.

Finally, I'd like to thank you for purchasing this book! If you found it helpful, I'd greatly appreciate it if you'd take a moment to leave a review on Amazon. Thank you!

Made in United States
Orlando, FL
20 July 2022

19971804R00026